AF426209

HISTORY OF SCOTLAND

A BRIEF HISTORY FROM BEGINNING TO END

HISTORY HUB

Bonus Downloads

*Get Free Books with **Any Purchase** History Hub*

Every purchase comes with a FREE download!

or Click Here.

Scan Your Phone to open QR code

History of Scotland

A Brief History from Beginning to the End

History Hub

© 2022 Copyright by History Hub. All Rights Reserved.

Please Note: The book you are about to enjoy is an analytical review meant for educational and entertainment purposes as an unofficial companion. If you have not yet read the original work, please do before purchasing this copy.

Disclaimer & Terms of Use: No part of this publication may be reproduced or retransmitted, electronic or mechanical, without the written permission of the publisher. The information in this book is meant for educational and entertainment purposes only and the publisher and author make no representations or warranties with respect to the accuracy or completeness of these contents and disclaim all warranties such as warranties of fitness for a particular purpose. Product names, logos, brands, and other trademarks featured or referred to within this publication are the property of their respective trademark holders and are not affiliated with this publication. This is an unofficial summary and analytical review meant for educational and entertainment purposes only and has not been authorized, approved, licensed, or endorsed by the original book's author or publisher and any of their licensees or affiliates.

CONTENTS

Chapter One
Introduction

The first recorded history of Scotland was during the first century AD, which formed part of the Roman invasion of Britain. The Romans were great record keepers and their scribes chronicled history in a way their subjects never would have done. The Romans incorporated the southern part of Britain into their empire under the name Brittania, but despite their military prowess, were unable to subdue the fierce tribes to the North who were never annexed to Roman Britain.

Roman Emperor Hadrian had a long, high wall built right across the country in an attempt to stop the Scottish warriors from invading Brittania. The central border with Scotland was fortified by the formidable Antonine Wall, and in fact, parts of Hadrian's wall can still be found today. The Romans called this land Caledonia and its people the Picts (from the Latin word to paint) because they painted their faces and bodies blue when they went to war.

In 800 AD, Scotland was invaded by the Vikings. They settled in the West of Scotland while the Picts began to develop the legendary Kingdom of Alba.

By the fifth century AD, the Celts from Ireland settled to the north of the River Clyde. These people were called Scots and they were Christian. In the sixth century, the Pict king was converted to Christianity. The Pict kingdom joined the Scots under the Scottish king, Kenneth MacAlpin in the ninth century, and by the tenth century, the land had become known as Scotland.

When the Normans invaded England in 1066, many of the Anglo Saxons moved into the Scottish lowlands, and the Lowland Scots adopted feudalism and other English ways, gradually becoming more Anglicized. The clan chiefs became nobles.

In 1040 AD, Macbeth ruled Scotland as the King of Alba for 17 years. This story was immortalized by William Shakespeare and shows how sophisticated the Scottish kingdom had become.

By the twelfth century, most of Scotland had become a feudal society. Only in the distant Highlands did the old clan still dominate.

During the Battle of Stirling Bridge, William Wallace, who made movie fame as *Braveheart*, saw the English being forced to retreat in 1297 from its attempt to become Scottish overlords.

In 1306, Robert the Bruce became King of Scotland, finally defeating the English, and in 1320, Scotland declared itself independent in the symbolic Declaration of Arbroath.

In 1542, Mary Queen of Scots presented a threat to the English throne, which had recently rejected Catholicism during the time of Henry VIII. Mary was executed at the command of Elizabeth I. Shortly after Mary was imprisoned, her son became James VI of Scotland and James I of England. This unification of the crowns consolidated English control over Scotland. In 1707, this was strengthened by the Act of Union, which placed a single Westminster-based parliament over both countries.

The Jacobite rising, which was ruthlessly crushed during the Battle of Culloden in 1746, as all *Outlander* fans would know, ended any chance of Catholic rule over Scotland and consequently any chance of independence.

The British Government recognized the Highlanders as a potential threat and began ruthlessly cleansing the Highlands, forbidding the wearing of tartan and removing all power from the Clan Chiefs.

The periods of Enlightenment and Industrialisation in the centuries which followed saw Scotland play key roles in science, art, literature, invention, and education.

Scotland remained firmly in the power of England, until 1999, when the Scottish parliament was reconvened after 300 years. In 2014, almost half the population voted to leave the UK, but the vote went for staying with England. The Scots, however, were firmly against leaving the EU, and with this came an increasing opposition to remaining part of Britain. As a result, a new referendum is planned for October 2023. Perhaps Scotland will finally be an independent sovereign state again.

In the chapters that follow, we will be examining the history of this fascinating country and the characters who defined its rise and fall. Scotland has always been of absolute fascination to historians, writers, filmmakers, and musicians. The strength and independence of the Scottish people have given them an almost mythical persona. When you read of or watch the brave Highlanders with their swirling kilts and rousing music,

it's hard to remember that this was also the home of rigid Presbyterianism

and conservatism. From here on, we will look at the Scots from prehistory

to modern-day football hooliganism, and while enjoying their colorful and

romantic past, we'll try to look at all aspects of this intriguing nation.

We'll start with a brief look into the world of prehistoric Scotland.

Chapter Two

Prehistoric Scotland

The prehistoric era was a very long time ago and quite a bit of the information we have is educated guesswork by historians, archeologists, and paleontologists based on their excavations. And of course, Scotland wasn't called Scotland until about 800 years ago so when we're talking about Scotland, we're talking about the land that is now called Scotland.

The Stone Age or Paleolithic period in Scotland began about 14 000 years ago. That was very recent compared with the evidence from Africa where early humans were using tools as far back as 2.5 million years ago. This probably occurred for two reasons. It's definite now that the cradle of mankind is in Africa and that people progressed from Africa outwards—it's a long way from Africa to Scotland. The other reason is that Scotland is cold and early man would probably have favored warmer climates. Scotland, until 14 000 years ago, was covered with ice sheets that made it largely uninhabitable as food would have been scarce. When a warmer period arose, around the time that evidence has been found of early habitation, hunter-gatherers would walk across from Europe in the warmer seasons and hunt or gather berries, roots, and other food types. The sea levels were lower then so it was possible to walk across land that is now submerged in the ocean.

During the Paleolithic, Mesolithic and Neolithic periods, which translate directly from Latin meaning Old, Middle, and New Stone Age, there was evidence that early man only used stone tools, hence the naming convention. Ancient stone tools were found in Scotland dating to this period and ending about 1000 years later. These tools have been found along rivers, on shores, and occasionally in caves, but it's fairly evident that these early people were not permanent settlers but migrants who traveled based on climatic conditions. A few sites show signs of short-term habitation, but early man probably preferred the warmer areas in what is now known as Southern Europe, as indeed do most holidaymakers today. There are no permanent sites that a tourist can visit showing that these early people had settled but some caves and rock shelters show evidence that a few intrepid souls lived in this harsh environment.

The Mesolithic period stretched from 10 800 BC to about 4 100 BC. (Of course, you know that BC means Before Christ or as it's now more popularly known, BCE - Before Common Era. This change is because BC and AD (Anno Domini) are explicitly Christian, which might seem a bit exclusive to other groups of people.) At this stage, people were still using wooden, stone, and bone tools, but as this period followed the end of the Ice Age when the climate improved, they could now fish and even clear land areas for agriculture. They even learned sophisticated techniques by using little flint implements to make sickles, spears and arrowheads. They also left evidence of building little timber structures that served as shelters, which meant they were around more permanently, at least during the summer. Evidence exists of antler bones being used as tools and of hazel nuts and fish being consumed. Scotland's acidic soil has not allowed much organic material to remain as evidence, but it's obvious that people were no longer just nomadic hunter-gatherers.

The Neolithic period ran from approximately 4100 BC and ended just 2500 years before Christ was born. This period showed early evidence of farming, and stone buildings, with some utilized as tombs, and ended with the use of copper tools, indicating early mining operations, possibly imported from Europe. This heralded the Bronze Age.

The Bronze Age ran from 2500 BC to 800 BC. Although the Copper Age in Europe was a period before the Iron Age, it's believed that by the time these metals arrived in Scotland, the technique of combining tin and copper to create the harder metal bronze was already in place, and Scotland might have missed the Copper Age altogether. There is a lot of Bronze Age evidence including the creation of jet, gold or amber jewelry and knives, and daggers, which indicated the beginning of social hierarchies. Stone burial chambers preserved and protected these sites and their artifacts.

The Iron Age arrived in Scotland about 2800 years ago and ended in approximately 400 AD. This was evidenced by iron tools for warfare and for agriculture. Evidence of carriages indicates that horses were probably important during these times. An abundance of forts were found from this time period as people, no longer hunter-gatherers or nomads, developed systems to protect themselves, their territory, and their possessions.

Chapter Three
The Arrival of the Romans and the Viking Invasions

The Romans

Scotland has always been of interest to invaders, and since early years have been forced to defend themselves and their independence.

The Romans arrived in Scotland soon after 70 AD and found a very hostile reception. After they had subdued the people of their new territory Britannica and brought them round to the advantages of Roman culture, ideas and Christianity, they turned their attention to the North where they found a very different reception.

The Romans originally built forts along Gask Ridge and the area which would become the Antonine Wall. The ongoing skirmishes eventually forced the Romans to withdraw, but in 142 AD, Antoninus built his magnificent Turf Wall. This was a bank, about 4 meters high, made of layers of turf surrounded by a wide ditch on the northside, and a military road on the south. In 65 AD, however, it was abandoned as the troops were pulled back to Hadrian's Wall.

This famous wall which was close to the current Scottish-English border ran from Wallsend 73 miles to Bowness on Solway. It took 6 years to build and was meant to keep the Scots in because they were so troublesome.

The Romans made several attempts to invade Scotland over the next century and some remains of their camps can be found as far north as Inverness and Aberdeen, but on the whole they gave it up as a bad job, and the Romans had never really entrenched the Scottish territory.

<u>The Norse/Vikings</u>

Around about 793 AD, the Scots fell victim to the Viking scourge as did England. These warlike Scandinavians, well documented in miniseries like *The Vikings,* waged a reign of terror on Scottish coastal towns until they gradually integrated into the local population. By 1000 AD, Viking raids had disappeared and the Viking settlers known as Norsemen assimilated the Scottish culture.

Some Scottish regions, like Shetland, actually remained under the rule of Norway and Denmark until 1472 AD during the late Medieval period.

Imagine the scene when the first Viking invaders arrived in Scotland in 793 AD. The Norsemen (Northmen) struck with a vengeance. People in fishing villages would see the mighty Viking boats with their fiercely painted dragon-like hulls and have little time to escape as the boats could travel at relatively high speeds, rowed by strong men with mighty muscles. The Vikings would have sent scouts a few days before to ensure that the villagers had no protection. The onslaught would have been sudden and fierce with all the men being violently killed and the women and children were taken hostage. Rape and pillage would have been inevitable, and the villages and crops would be destroyed by fire so that any escapees had no home to return to. The Norsemen believed in a vindictive crew of gods led by Odin. They had no fear of death believing they would feast in Valhalla if they were courageous and fearless. They had no respect for the pacifistic Christian religion and particularly enjoyed attacking monasteries that had a great deal of treasure.

It's not surprising that the Scots in later history, with the combination of Viking and Pict blood, proved to be such fierce opposition to any form of attack and so resistant to giving up their independence. It's also interesting to note the people who lived in Scotland were descendants of the Picts, the Irish Celts, and the Vikings.

The early Medieval period covers this period in history, as the Iron Age gave way to early Christian Scotland. The Medieval period itself began about 800 AD and ended a mere 500 years ago. In the early Medieval period, Scotland was divided into a number of kingdoms between the end of the Roman influence and the rise of the Kingdom of Alba in about 900 BC.

Because of the country's extensive coastline and huge areas of land which were difficult to access and nearly impossible to farm, the human settlement remained light compared to more fertile and accessible areas in England. Farming remained largely self-sufficient, and life expectancy was low so the population was relatively young with a ruling aristocracy, a small number of free men and a large number of slaves. The many languages gradually gave way to Gaelic, and several kings surrounded by their war bands kept up almost constant squabbles and skirmishes. Although this time was classified as the Scottish Dark Ages, it was still a time of social, literary, and artistic growth.

Chapter Four
The Courageous Tale of William Wallace

By the end of the 10th century, Scotland had adopted its current name and was becoming less warlike and remote, especially in the South. After the Norman invasion in 1066, the South became increasingly Anglicized and the English monarchy tightened its grip on Scotland. The remote North remained largely unaffected, but rebellious Scottish nobles in the Southern areas, particularly where the Lowlands meet the Highlands, resented English control. This situation culminated in the Battle of Stirling Bridge in 1297.

It was masterminded by the famous struggle hero William Wallace, a knight who epitomized the sacrifice and struggle that the Scots were prepared to undergo to overthrow their English oppressors. He remains a national hero to this day and is, of course, immortalized by Mel Gibson in the film *Braveheart.*

He was born in 1270 AD and was raised as a minor noble. His father was a knight and vassal of James Stewart, the Scottish High Steward. Young William was born an outlaw because his father refused to sign his name on the Ragman Rolls of 1296 where Scottish nobles pledged their allegiance to King Edward and the English Crown.

Edward I of England, or Edward Longshanks as he was known, was impressively tall for that day and age and was a seasoned hotheaded warrior who set his sights on Scotland again. Scotland was going through a succession crisis. Alexander III had died without living children, and his successor was his granddaughter, Margaret the Maid of Norway, who died on the voyage from France. The nobles jostled for power and finally asked Edward I to choose a ruler for them. Edward I chose an ineffectual puppet ruler called John Balliol who ruled for a mere 4 years. The frustrated nobles began to turn to Robert the Bruce, grandfather of his more famous namesake for rule and guidance.

The Scottish nobility was fed up with the weak rule of Balliol whom they soon realized had no concern for the Scottish people but was just there to implement Edward I's harsh laws and punitively high taxes, which he was using to fund his French wars. In 1290, Scotland allied itself to France, and even Balliol revoked his allegiance to Edward I. Edward I retaliated by marching on the town of Berwick and slaughtering 11 060 innocent souls. The Bruces, who had never supported Balliol and the Auld Alliance with

France, rallied to the King's aid, and Balliol was defeated and condemned to imprisonment in the Tower of London. The Scottish monarchy effectively ended as Edward I put three English barons in charge of Scotland. He even stole the famous Stone of Scone, the symbol of Scottish monarchy, and put it in Westminster Abbey.

The rebellious William Wallace and a small band of rebels started attacking groups of British nobles, ostensibly in revenge for an attack on his sweetheart and for the massacre of Scottish nobles. Successful attacks were made in Lanark where an English sheriff was killed and in Scone and several other garrisons. Wallace and his rebel band fled to the safety of the Highlands but on 11 September 1297, he successfully attacked and routed the much stronger English army at Stirling Bridge. While history is shaky on the details, it appears that Wallace declared that he was determined to regain Scottish independence and that at least 100 English knights were killed. It's the stuff of legend that the bridge collapsed and the knights drowned, weighed down by their heavy armor. One particularly gruesome detail was that following the death of Edward I's Treasurer, Sir Hugh de Cressingham, his skin was flayed and dried to make sporrans and sword belts for the Scottish victors.

William Wallace continued his attacks on the English and became increasingly bold, receiving Royal favor from Robert the Bruce and was made Guardian of Scotland and commander in chief of the Scottish armed forces.

The Battle of Falkirk of 1298, led by Edward I himself, proved the undoing of Wallace's successful reign of terror. The Scottish spearsmen were routed by the English cavalry and the feared longbows. In the battle's aftermath, 20 000 Scots fell to the 2000 English. Wallace and most of the Scottish nobles escaped, but the defeat was ignominious, and Wallace had to resign as Guardian of Scotland.

Robert the Bruce had a definite tendency to vacillate. When his daughter married an ally of Edward I's and Balliol was released from the tower, Robert the Bruce found himself on the English side again. He had definite aspirations for the crown of Scotland and chose his allies accordingly.

Wallace remained on the run, but according to legend, was finally betrayed by friends and captured in 1305. A whole range of charges was brought against him from murder to treason, and he was sentenced to the horrific death of being hanged, drawn, and quartered. On 23 August, he was dragged behind a horse by his heels through the streets of London.

After which he was hanged until almost dead, then his stomach was cut open, his intestines removed, and finally he was decapitated and his body cut into four quarters. Each quarter was dispatched to a part of Scotland and put on public display as a warning to those who wished to embark on treason against the English Crown. Wallace has remained one of the great figures of Scottish history and great statues of William Wallace and Robert the Bruce stand side by side at the gatehouse of Edinburgh Castle, protectors of the Scots.

A metal sculpture of a viking longboat on the Stonehaven boardwalk. Around about 793 AD, the Scots fell victim to the Viking scourge as did England. These warlike Scandinavians conducted a reign of terror on Scottish coastal towns until they gradually integrated into the local populations.

The great statues of William Wallace and Robert the Bruce stand side by side at the gatehouse of Edinburgh Castle, protectors of the Scots.

Chapter Five
Robert the Bruce 1274-1329

Section 1 Robert the Bruce - The Early Years

Like many of the Scottish nobles during this troubled time, Robert the Bruce suffered a great deal of hardship. He was born a minor noble, distantly related to the Scottish Royal Family. When the puppet king John Balliol broke away from his allegiance to Edward I and was declared king by the Scottish nobility, the Bruce family refused to acknowledge him and supported Edward I. This naturally led to England's control of Scotland again. The Bruces were ambitious and had an eye on the throne. When William Wallace was defeated, Edward I did not confiscate Robert the Bruce's lands, and he became Guardian of Scotland with Balliol's nephew John Comyn. Theirs was a volatile relationship and after a quarrel, Robert the Bruce stabbed Comyn in a church in Dumfries. Because churches were holy ground, this was a great sacrilege and Robert the Bruce was excommunicated by the Pope and outlawed by Edward I.

Section 2 Robert the Bruce and the Spider

Ignoring this, Robert the Bruce declared himself King in 1306 and was crowned on 26 March. He was deposed the following year, and his wife and daughters were imprisoned while three of his brothers were executed. Fortunately for him, Edward Longshanks died in 1306, and his son Edward II was an utterly useless soldier, so Robert the Bruce was able to win back castle after castle from the English, particularly after his great victory at Bannockburn in 1314. Robert the Bruce remains one of the great national heroes, finally bringing independence to Scotland in 1328.

One of the favorite stories about Robert the Bruce is very well known by every school child in Scotland.

On one occasion when Robert the Bruce was on the run from the English, he sheltered in a cave. Feeling very disheartened and ready to give up, he looked up and saw a spider trying to build her web on the slippery wall of the cave. She had obviously chosen a spot where a small chink of light would lure moths and similar insects, but it was a tricky spot to build on. Again and again, the little spider failed, but finally, the web held, and she was able to build her home and find a stable source of food. Robert the

Bruce took great comfort in this, and it motivated him to try again to defeat the English and secure the independence of his beloved Scotland.

Section 3 The tragic end of Robert the Bruce.

Despite his 26 years as a great king, Robert the Bruce had a rather ignominious end, possibly dying of leprosy on 7 June 1329. Leprosy held a great stigma in those days, and the jury is still out on whether the great king actually had this pariah's disease or not.

While his body's final resting place was at Dunfermline Abbey, his heart was placed in a cone-shaped casket and taken on a crusade to Spain. His heart was later brought back for burial in Melrose Abbey. Thus both the body and heart of this great king of Scotland were laid to rest in the land that he spent his life defending.

Chapter Six
Scotland from 1329 to 1542

Section 1 - Two Hundred Years of Stewart Rule

<u>1371-89 Robert II.</u> Robert II was the son of Princess Marjorie Bruce, Robert the Bruce's daughter. He was 55 when he finally ascended the throne. He married his mistress, Elizabeth, and then, after her death, Lady Euphemia of Ross. Unfortunately, there were always succession questions based on the legitimacy of his first marriage.

<u>1390-1406 Robert III.</u> This unfortunate king had a history of failure before he even started his reign. The son of Robert II and his first wife Elizabeth, his right to the throne was questioned because the legitimacy of his parent's marriage was doubted. He was an ineffective administrator. He allowed his brother Robert Stewart increasing control, which led to increasing rivalry. His own sons were victims of this power play when his son David was murdered under suspicious circumstances, and his younger son James was intercepted by the English while being sent to safety and was taken prisoner. This was the last straw for the troubled

king who sank into a terrible depression, feeling, probably quite rightfully, that his reign was a failure.

1406-37 James I. James I, who was captured at the age of 12 while in transit to France, was held by the English until age twenty after his father's death. He had married a cousin of Henry VI of England, Joan Beaufort, which put him in royal favor and was finally allowed to return to his homeland for an extortionate ransom of £40,000. He and Joan had 8 children. He promptly dispatched of any rivals, murdering Murdoch Stewart who had ruled while he was in exile, and his two sons. Despite his strong leadership, the legitimacy claims, which stemmed from his grandfather's first marriage came to haunt him too. He was challenged by the descendants of the second marriage, and he was murdered in his royal lodgings on the command of Walter Stewart, one of the claimants.

1437-60 James II. James II was born a twin, who inherited the throne at the tender age of seven and died young. He had a fiery birthmark on his face, which kept him out of the public eye, but he made up for this by becoming a fierce warrior. He married in 1449 and had 7 children. His reign was as bloody as the rest. As a young child, he became embroiled in a battle with rival claimants and eventually stabbed an unrepentant rival to death and threw him through the castle window. He himself was killed by an exploding cannon while he was siding with the House of Lancaster during the War of Roses.

1460-88 James III. James III was nine when he came to the throne. He was abducted, as a child, and forced to marry Princess Margaret of Denmark. Although a patron of the arts and, almost definitely of homosexual tendencies, he tended to let his affection for all his young courtiers get the better of him. He was eventually murdered after his own young son James IV was abducted and led to battle against him. James IV apparently wore an iron link belt as penance for his part in his father's demise.

1488-1513 James IV. Poor James IV, despite his terrible ordeal witnessing his father's death, was a great success as a king, stabilizing the economy and vastly improving education. He was very well educated himself, speaking 8 languages. He married Princess Margaret Tudor, daughter of Henry VII when his mistress, whom he intended to marry, was found poisoned. He died in 1513 at the Battle of Flodden defending his old allies in France against the English Spanish Alliance.

<u>1513-42 James V.</u> James V was just seventeen months old when he came to the throne. By the time he was able to rule, he was closely allied with Catholic France through his marriage and treaties, despite his mother being the aunt of Henry VIII, who tried to persuade him to accept his protestant reforms. James V refused and relationships soured with the English once again invading Scotland and defeating them. James V died from illness soon after this.

Section 2 - Mary Queen of Scots 1542-87

Scotland had a queen. On the death of James V, his six-day-old daughter Mary was declared queen.

Fortunately, King Henry VIII, being highly superstitious, believed that he had been cursed by his nephew's death, so he did not follow up on his victory against Scotland, instead agreeing that the infant Queen of Scots should be betrothed to his son Edward.

Unfortunately, the unscrupulous Cardinal Beaton collaborated with the French and scrapped the treaty by arranging a betrothal with Francis, Dauphin of France, son of the ruthless Catherine de' Medici and Henry II. In retaliation, England invaded Scotland, Cardinal Beaton was murdered and the Scots were roundly punished. In 1547, Henry VIII died and six-year-old Queen Mary was taken to safety at the French Court. This is another story immortalized in film in the series *Reign.*

Section 3 - The Tumultuous Reign of Mary

Mary is probably the best-known character in Scotland's troubled royal history. The young Queen was forced to return to Scotland after her husband Francis, Dauphin of France, died still in his teens.

She found Scotland very rough after the elegance of the French Court. Scotland had followed England in its Catholic-Protestant split and so a Protestant husband, Lord Darnley was chosen for Mary. Strong-willed Mary had no time for her weak husband who soon became a drunkard. He became jealous of his beautiful wife and murdered her favorite courtier Riccio when she was 6 months pregnant. When her son James VI was born, she had him baptized Catholic causing alarm among the Protestant groupings.

In 1567, Lord Darnley was suspiciously murdered when his lodgings blew up one night. He was found, however, to have been strangled. Mary, still young and beautiful became involved with James Hepburn, Earl of Bothwell, who was accused of Lord Darnley's murder but acquitted. Mary married the Earl of Bothwell but this decision enraged the Lords of

Congregation who imprisoned her in Lochleven Castle, where as a result

of this trauma, she gave birth to stillborn twins. The Earl of Bothwell fled

and Mary never saw him again. He died, insane in Denmark. Mary escaped

Lochleven Castle and attempted to muster an army but was defeated by

the Protestants and was forced to flee to England. She abdicated in 1568.

Are You Enjoying Reading?

As an independent publisher

with a tiny marketing budget

we rely on readers, like you.

Click here to a brief review on Amazon

If you're receiving help from this book,

would you please take a moment to write a brief review?

We really appreciate it.

Simply scan QR Code with your Smartphone

Chapter Seven
Mary and Elizabeth

Section 1 - The Rival Cousins

The relationship between Mary and her cousin Elizabeth I of England never really stood a chance. Although they were both lonely young queens, Mary, with her very strong claim, not only to the Scottish but also to the English throne at a time of religious turmoil, was simply too great a threat for Protestant Elizabeth I to ignore, especially since she was unwed and without heirs. It is possible that she felt some sympathy for her dispossessed cousin, having herself been in semi-imprisonment and called a bastard, but her own needs proved greater, and Elizabeth I remained a harsh and unforgiving cousin to poor Mary. It probably did not help that Mary was young and beautiful and already had a son who was a potential heir to the throne of England.

Section 2 - The Long Imprisonment

When Mary fled to England, she might have expected mercy from her Royal cousin but received none. From the very beginning, Elizabeth I's advisors urged her to execute her cousin but Elizabeth I, like her father

Henry VIII was superstitious about spilling Royal blood, so she imprisoned her in many castles for nearly nineteen long years. She stayed in Carlisle Castle where she was permitted to walk with her retinue outside the castle walls. She also stayed for long periods at Wingfield Manor, Hardwick Hall, and Chatsworth House, all belonging to the Earl of Shrewsbury who remained her chief captor. His wife Bess would sew and embroider with Mary, and much of that beautiful work is still on show today in these stately homes.

Of course, the still young and spirited Mary hated her captivity and wrote copious letters of complaint begging to be treated better. These were largely ignored. Mary finally got herself into trouble when she conspired to escape with Anthony Babington who had admired her since he was a young boy. As a young courtier, he had apparently stained his face with walnut juice, so he could escape detection when visiting Mary. After her attempt to escape with Babington, she also tacitly agreed to plot against Elizabeth I, which was her undoing. She was accused of treason, and Elizabeth I had no option but to act against her.

Section 3 - Death at the Executioner's Block

Elizabeth I reluctantly signed her cousin's death warrant once she was found guilty of treason. On 17 February, 1587, Mary was executed at Fotheringhay Castle where it is said it took three blows from the executioner's ax to finally sever her head. On an even more gruesome note, according to legend, when her head was lifted by the hair to show to the crowd, her wig was left in the executioner's hand, and her head rolled away. Mary was buried at Peterborough Cathedral. Her friend Babington was also gruesomely executed by being hanged, drawn, and quartered.

Later, when her son James VI came to power, he moved his mother's body to Westminster Abbey and laid her to rest in a tomb that was definitely larger and more prominent than that of Elizabeth I.

Robert the Bruce 1274-1329.

After his death, his body was buried at Dunfermline Abbey, but his heart was placed in a cone-shaped casket and taken on a crusade to Spain. His heart was later brought back for burial in Melrose Abbey. Thus, both the body and heart of this great king of Scotland were laid to rest in the land that he spent his life defending.

Mary, Queen of Scots wearing white as a symbol of mourning. This display was to honor the death of three family members who were lost over a period eighteen months.

Chapter Eight
James the First of England

Section 1 - The Orphan Prince

James VI of Scotland was born in 1566. His father Lord Darnley was murdered when he was only eight months old, and his mother Mary Queen of Scots abdicated, making him king when he was only one year old. His mother fled to England the following year, and the baby Prince never saw her again. James VI was raised by a group of great Scottish lords, and he was grateful his whole life for their care and support. They raised him as young Medieval princes were always raised—with a good education in languages, law, astronomy, and the arts of warfare. This had the effect of making him very pedantic, and this fact about him annoyed people his whole life. His self-confidence meant that by the age of 12, he insisted on having a significant role in governing the country, which was still ruled by factions and intriguers. He decided early to seek union with England rather than animosity.

Section 2 - The Union of the Crown

James the VI of Scotland, having decided that he wanted to follow Elizabeth I on the throne of England, in a sense set himself up to neglect his own people. One easy way he had done this was when he became a Protestant himself, and by 1584, he was firmly placed as head of the Presbyterian church in Scotland despite his mother's loyalty to her Catholic faith to the end. His ambition caused him to make only a token protest when his mother was executed.

James VI succeeded Elizabeth I in 1603 and ascended to the English throne as James I. From the very beginning, he found the sophisticated English parliament a far cry from the more naive and amenable Scottish one, and his 22-year reign was affected by his narrow vision and pedantic nature.

Section 3 - The End of Scottish Independence

The success of James I on the thrones of both England and Scotland effectively disadvantaged Scotland. James I was so busy with English foreign policy and with his own problems with the arrogance of the English parliament who disrespected him for his pompous lectures and lack of physical attractiveness. They found him to be an embarrassing king and found his policies to be out of line with their own, so they thwarted him at every turn. Rebellion among the ranks of his ministers made James I's reign a hard one, and with parliament often refusing to fund his projects, he became unpopular with the people as he taxed them more heavily. His son and heir Charles, in later years, turned against his father, particularly because James I kept trying to force alliances with England's mortal enemy, Spain.

By the time James I died, his son Charles and his advisors were firmly in control. It's no wonder that Scotland was sorely neglected by the man who was first and foremost their king. However, the one thing that James I did achieve is the overseeing of the first English Bible called the King James Bible, a name it holds to this day and is still much loved by traditionalists.

Chapter Nine
The Jacobite Rising

Section 1 - Who were the Jacobites?

The largely uneventful Stuart rule, which followed Tudor rule, lasted from James I in 1603 to Queen Anne whose reign ended in 1714. The Stuart kings and queens Charles I, Charles II, James II, William III, and Mary II ruled for over 100 years. The end of Stuart rule caused major drama in Scotland, which finally broke the last vestiges of Scottish independence.

King George I of the House of Hanover caused the end of Stuart rule. The Jacobites were a political organization in Scotland, the North of England, and Ireland who wished to see the Stuart Kings, in the person of the father of Bonnie Prince Charlie, restored to the English throne. Catholicism was still outlawed, and Catholics supported the Jacobite movement because they wanted a Catholic king on the throne.

The Jacobite Rebellion of 1715, which followed the Revolution of 1688, ended the Catholic line of the Stuart dynasty. The Jacobites had actively rebelled since.

Political disarray in England between the Tories and the Whigs when King George came to the throne meant that the Jacobites could take the opportunity to rebel. George I quickly quelled the rebellion in England but was less successful in Scotland. The Earl of Mar escaped to the Highlands and raised the Jacobite flag in Braemar

Section 2 - Bonnie Prince Charlie

Bonnie Prince Charlie or Charles Edward Stuart was born in exile in Rome in 1730. As a descendent of the exiled Catholic Stuarts, he and his followers believed that his line should be on the throne, particularly since his claim was endorsed by the Pope who had given them home and protection in Rome.

In 1744, with the support of France, Bonnie Prince Charlie planned to sail a fleet across the English Channel to claim his throne, but a severe storm stopped this attempt. In 1745, Charlie, as Prince regent, was determined to return the throne to his father, so he arrived on the Isle of Eriskay after hearing that he had strong Highland support. However, the promised French support never reached them. He had never been to England let alone Scotland. One can only wonder what he thought of the Highlands compared to Rome where he had been raised.

The Battle of Prestonpans was a great victory by the Jacobite forces led by Bonnie Prince Charlie against government forces.

Section 3 - The Tragedy of Culloden

While Bonnie Prince Charlie initially went South to seek support, he found little popularity in the territory, so he returned to Scotland. On 16 April 1746, he led the Highland troops to battle on the Culloden fields near Inverness. The scenes from the popular series *Outlander* give one a perfect example of the horrors of the battle. Bonnie Prince Charlie made a strategic error when planning the battle, and the Jacobites were destroyed within an hour. As many as 2000 men lost their lives, and many others were captured. Bonnie Prince Charlie returned to Rome where he lived until his death, but this uprising effectively was the death warrant for the Highland clans.

Chapter Ten

The End of the Clans

Section 1 - The Cleansing of the Highlands

The Highland clans from the far North of Scotland were the last remains of the ancient clan system. *Clann* is a Gaelic word meaning children, and all members of a clan felt a strong sense of loyalty and duty to one another. The Highland clearances started after the Battle of Culloden and lasted for over a hundred years as they were systematically dispossessed of their land, their culture, and their way of life. It also led to the emigration of Scots to other countries across the world.

By the mid-1800s, there was a definite divide between the south of Scotland, which saw itself as progressive and modern and similar to its English neighbors, and the fierce and proud clansmen of the Highlands whom they saw as backward and old fashioned.

After 1725, garrisons of Redcoats were set up all over Scotland with the brief to control the clans and break the power of their chieftains over them, reminding them that they were English subjects.

Section 2 - Cruel Oppression

After the Jacobite rebellions, laws were passed to break the power of the clans. In 1747, a cruel act banned the wearing of the clan tartan and the playing of the bagpipes. Furthermore, the teaching of gaelic was outlawed. This was a deliberate attempt to break the traditions and culture of the clans and destroy the clan's way of life. Severe punishment, flogging, imprisonment, and death enforced these laws.

The clans were also systematically dispossessed of their lands and forced to scrape living on the infertile and insufficient land made available to them. Prominent landowners took over Highlanders' land for commercial sheep farming, forcing them into subsistence fishing and kelp farming. This followed periods of great hardship, famine, and starvation. The proud landowners became impoverished crofters. Sadly enough, it's only in recent decades that history has been taken to task for this terrible oppression, but the bitterness it caused has remained entrenched to this day.

Section 3 - Tartan for Tourists

Nowadays, everybody who has a link to Scotland likes to visit the Highlands and buy themselves a clan kilt. Original kilts look nothing like the tailored items one can buy today and were not made in definitive patterns as they were dyed with plant material rather than woven into specific designs. The differences in color were probably meant to stop one from accidentally killing one's friends in battle. Women did not wear kilts either. They wore appropriate long dresses.

Kilts and tartan, in general, are one of the biggest draw cards for tourists to the Highlands, and most Scots seem to ignore cultural appropriation as long as it's done respectfully and correctly. They are not as prickly as other cultures seem to have become. It is, however, likely that a big guy from America wearing a bright red kilt and the tartan of his great great grandfather and having his Stetson hat on his head might draw some amused snickers from the locals. But still, it's tourism. Each to their own.

A portrait of Bonnie Prince Charlie (Charles Edward Stuart) done by William Mosman.

The Tartan of Charles Edward Stuart.

Chapter Eleven
The Return of the Scots

Scottish independence is an idea that is gaining ground in Scotland. *Unthirldom* is the Scottish word for independence, and it embraces the idea of an independent Scotland that is a sovereign state completely free from the control and influence of the UK. Of course, this has certain implications for freedom of movement, freedom to work, border controls, and trade controls. It is likely, however, that they would just have a soft border as they have with the Republic of Ireland, etc. The implications of this have been seen when the Scots were forced to join the UK in leaving the EU, which they did not want to do and voted against. This would undoubtedly have some influence on their finally leaving the UK. At least they could join the EU again.

There have been various campaigns for the self-government of Scotland since the early 19th century. These have largely wanted home rule under the auspices of the UK national government. In 1979 and again in 1997, referendums for devolution were held. A devolved Scottish parliament was eventually set up in 1999.

The party that steered this whole development is the Scottish National Party, and it has governed the devolved parliament since 2007. In 2014, the UK government agreed to abide by the results of a referendum asking the people of Scotland if they wanted independence from the UK. The results were close, but 55% of voters opted to stay with the UK. This must have been a disappointment to the governing party. However, the Scottish referendum on EU membership went strongly in favor of staying, unlike the vote in Britain, and it is probable that the next independence referendum planned for October 2023 is likely to go in favor of Scottish independence.

It is interesting, however, that despite centuries of war and seemingly desperate attempts to escape the English yoke, that when the actual crunch time came, the Scots did not all choose to be free of British rule. It's obvious that the Scottish people themselves have mixed feelings. During the 2014 referendum, both sides, *Yes Scotland* and *Better Together* argued their cases strongly. A number of important issues were raised including leaving the EU, the ownership of the North Sea Oil and the financial cost of independence. Strangely enough, when the public were questioned afterwards, one of the main sways for people voting against devolution was the risk of losing the pound sterling as their currency. Those who voted yes claimed a lack of faith in Westminster and its politics. This smacks very strongly of the disaffection that the Scots have always had for Westminster rule. Westminster is a long way from Scotland. It will be very interesting to see if the Scots will finally regain their hard-fought independence in 2023, or whether this is no longer an issue of such great consequence, and they will be happy to stay as a member of the UK. At least the choice will be theirs and will not be forced on them as it was so often in the past.

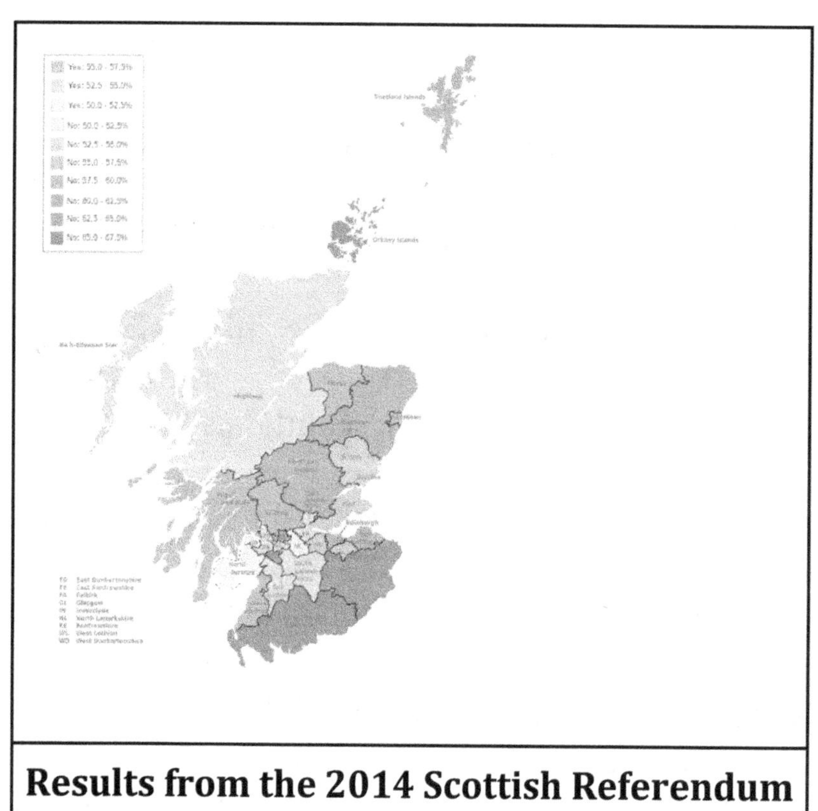

Results from the 2014 Scottish Referendum

Chapter Twelve
Conclusion

The history of Scotland is undoubtedly a fascinating one, but it's also one that holds a great number of questions for the nation's future.

The Scots retain a huge amount of deeply embedded national pride and a strong sense of their own history. It goes without saying that English attempts at colonialism throughout the world have had the effect of raising the ire of the nations they colonized and dividing the people within them into those that identified with English culture and those who felt their own culture had been marginalized. In Scotland this is not exactly the case; Scottish culture remains strong among the Scots, and there is a consistent rejection of English traditions and celebrations in favor of Scottish ones. Of course, there is a considerable amount of shared history so there are strong similarities in values, education, and certain forms of government, like democracy.

On the other hand, the Scots have always favored a more localized form of governance, which allows the involvement of centralized government but favors the diffusion of power. For this reason, the relations between

Scotland and England remain rather unstable, much as they always have. The future of their shared relationship as one nation is by no means definite. As we have examined in Section 10, the Scots have increasingly sought independence in their local rule, though fortunately, not by waging wars but through referendums.

We have also learned to ask some relevant questions about the nature of our own lives by studying the history of others. The study of history is always relevant because all of us are living through history every day. Each law passed, each riot, each pandemic, and each government change will eventually make it into the history books. It's also interesting to note that a synopsis of history usually makes it sound much more gory and horrible than it really was. For each incidence of war, death, or violence, there would have been many days of peaceful activities like eating, sleeping, celebrating, working on one's daily activities, and just generally living life.

By the study of history, we learn lessons that can inform our decisions and thus, avoid the mistakes of those who have gone before us. We can see the terrible effects of religious intolerance and of colonization and of human greed. We can see the positive effects of study, enlightenment, education and experimentation. We can also see the patterns emerging from the decisions several generations have made. We have benefited from the industrialization of our world through the inventions of earlier generations, but we have also created an environmental time bomb that the next generations will blame us for in the history books and will be tasked with correcting that balance again.

The history of Scotland is a particularly entertaining and colorful one, and it's to be hoped that the next time you sing *Auld Lang Syne* in the New Year or hold a Hogmanay party, you will remember William Wallace, Robert the Bruce, Mary Queen of Scots, and Bonnie Prince Charlie and be glad to know a little more about them.

Chapter Thirteen
Discussion Question

Primitive man emerged from Africa nearly 2 million years before he appeared in Scotland. What reasons might exist for the slower emergence of primitive man into Scotland? You can bear in mind the effects of the climate in your answer.

Discussion Question

Scotland appears to have missed the emergence of the Copper Age, going straight from Stone to Bronze. What reasons can you give for this? Share your thoughts.

Discussion Question

Why do you think it was so important to have a king physically present in Scotland? Look at the reign of James I as an example. Now discuss.

Discussion Question

Why did Robert the Bruce keep changing his allegiance between England and Scotland? How did it serve his ambitions? How might a single alliance have better served him?

Discussion Question

Why was Elizabeth I so nervous about her cousin Mary Queen of Scots? What did she fear from her? Do you think her fears were rational? Discuss.

Discussion Question

How did religion play a significant role in the way Scottish history played out? Do you think it was the most significant factor in all the dramas? Yes or no? Share the reason for your answer.

Discussion Question

What features of Scottish Highland culture do you find particularly attractive? Do you, like the English, find them a rather backward crowd? Yes or No? Discuss why you feel this way.

Discussion Question

Scotland has a wonderful, rich history. Which part of Scottish history did you find most interesting? Please complement your response with examples explaining why you feel as you do.

Chapter Fourteen
Quiz Question

1. **True/False:** The name Scotland originally came from the Pict people. They were amongst the earliest settlers in the area. This probably explains why they gave their name to Scotland.

2. **True/False:** MacBeth was king of Scotland in the eleventh century. His story always seems quite mythical. His story was fictionalized in a play by William Shakespeare.

3. **True/False:** Robert the Bruce was apparently encouraged by watching the attempts of a little mouse to escape through a hole. He was hiding from the English. The little creature gave him strength to persevere.

4. **True/False:** Mary Queen of Scots was originally married to the Dauphin of France who was the son of Catherine de' Medici. The French Dauphin was named Francis. He was the love of Mary's life.

5. **True/ False:** James I of England was the mentor and encouragement behind the translating of the Bible into English. His name was given to it and remains today. It is particularly loved by traditionalists.

6. **True/False:** Bonnie Prince Charlie did eventually succeed to the English throne after a lot of disappointments. He defeated the English. He reinstated the Stuart line.

7. **True/False:** The Highlanders were banned from wearing tartan and playing bagpipes. They were, however, still allowed to speak Gaelic. They were allowed to stay on their extensive lands.

8. **True/ False:** The Scottish people agreed with the English voters. They voted in favor of leaving the EU. This was very surprising because the Scots seldom agree with the English.

Quiz Answer

1. False, they were Celts from Ireland

2. True

3. False, it was a spider spinning a web.

4. True

5. True

6. . False, he returned to Rome and there were never any Stuarts on the throne again.

7. False, they were banned from speaking Gaelic too and were evicted from their lands.

8. False, they voted not to leave the EU.

Bonus Downloads

*Get Free Books with **Any Purchase** History Hub*

Every purchase comes with a FREE download!

or Click Here.

Scan Your Phone to open QR code

Thank You For Reading

As an independent publisher

with a tiny marketing budget

we rely on readers, like you.

Click here to a brief review on Amazon

If you're receiving help from this book,

would you please take a moment to write a brief review?

We really appreciate it.

Simply scan QR Code with your Smartphone

www.ingramcontent.com/pod-product-compliance
Lightning Source LLC
Chambersburg PA
CBHW080943120726
48003CB00011B/3269